LIVELY DISCUSSIONS!
FOSTERING ENGAGED READING

Linda B. Gambrell
University of Maryland
College Park, Maryland

Janice F. Almasi
State University of New York at Buffalo
Buffalo, New York

Editors

INTERNATIONAL READING ASSOCIATION
800 Barksdale Road, PO Box 8139
Newark, Delaware 19714-8139, USA

The International Reading Association attempts, through its publications, to provide a forum for a wide spectrum of opinions on reading. This policy permits divergent viewpoints without implying the endorsement of the Association.

Director of Publications   Joan M. Irwin
Assistant Director of Publications   Wendy Lapham Russ
Senior Editor   Christian A. Kempers
Associate Editor   Matthew W. Baker
Assistant Editor   Janet S. Parrack
Editorial Assistant   Cynthia C. Sawaya
Production Department Manager   Iona Sauscermen
Graphic Design Coordinator   Boni Nash
Design Consultant   Larry F. Husfelt
Desktop Publishing Supervisor   Wendy A. Mazur
Desktop Publisher   Anette Schütz-Ruff
Desktop Publisher   Cheryl J. Strum
Production Services Editor   David K. Roberts

Photo Credits: Jan Doyle, cover; Robert Finken, pgs. 1, 51, 249; Michael Siluk pg. 169.

Library of Congress Cataloging in Publication Data
    Lively discussions!:Fostering engaged reading/Linda B. Gambrell and Janice F. Almasi, editors.
        p.   cm.
    Includes bibliographical references and index.
    1. Forums (Discussion and debate)   2. Reading (Elementary)   3. Literature—Study and teaching (Elementary)   4. Group reading.   I. Gambrell, Linda B.   II. Almasi, Janice F.
LC6551.L58   1996   96-17614
372.41—dc20
ISBN 0-87207-147-2
Third Printing, April 2000

CONTENTS

PART III: CREATING THE CLIMATE: THE ROLE OF THE TEACHER

PART IV: PERSPECTIVES ON ASSESSING DISCUSSIONS

ABOUT THE AUTHORS

Jeanette Allison is an assistant professor in the College of Education at Arizona State University West, Phoenix, Arizona, USA. Her career began as a teacher of preschool and primary-age children in California, Oregon, and Illinois. She earned a doctorate degree in early childhood education from the University of Illinois at Urbana-Champaign. She teaches courses on early education and literacy, and works with inner-city and minority children. Her research helps teachers create cultures of achievement with the use of inquiry learning, projects, and multiple texts. Her work has been published in *The Reading Teacher, Educational Leadership*, and *Childhood Education*.

Janice F. Almasi is a former classroom teacher and reading specialist. She is currently assistant professor of reading at the State University of New York at Buffalo, Buffalo, New York, USA, and is affiliated with the National Reading Research Center at the Universities of Maryland and Georgia. Her research focuses on patterns of social interaction, discourse, engagement, and cognitive processing during peer discussions of literature. She was awarded the International Reading Association's Outstanding Dissertation of the Year Award in 1994 and the National Reading Conference's Outstanding Student Research Award in 1993. Her work has been published in *Reading Research Quarterly, The Journal of Reading Behavior*, and *Educational Psychologist*.

Shelby J. Barrentine has taught in elementary schools in the U.S. for over ten years. Currently, she is an assistant professor of elementary education in the Center for Teaching and Learning at the University of North Dakota, Grand Forks, North Dakota, USA. She teaches graduate and undergraduate courses in literacy teaching and learning. She is especially interested in the study of read-aloud events in elementary school classrooms and in language-based thematic teaching.

Trevor H. Cairney is an English educator with over 25 years' experience in schools and universities. He has been at the University of Western Sydney, Australia, for seven years, spending five years as dean of education before beginning his current appointment as university pro vice-chancellor (research). He is the past president of the Australian Literacy Educators' Association and director of the New South Wales Children's Literacy & ESL Research Network. He has conducted 19 funded research projects and published the results of his work in over 100 publications. He has written eight books, the most recent being *Other Worlds: The Endless Possibilities of Literature* (Heinemann), *Teaching Reading Comprehension: Meaning Makers at Work* (Open University Press), *Beyond Tokenism: Parents as Partners in Literacy Learning* (Heinemann), and *Pathways to Literacy* (Cassell).

Michelle Commeyras has taught in elementary schools, junior and senior high schools, and most recently at the college level. She has a master's degree in critical and creative thinking from the University of Massachusetts, Boston. In 1991, she received a Ph.D. in education from the University of Illinois at Urbana-Champaign. She presently teaches in the Department of Reading Education at the University of Georgia, Athens, Georgia, USA, and conducts research for the National Reading Research Center.

Linda B. Gambrell is the associate dean for research in the College of Education at the University of Maryland, College Park, Maryland, USA, where she teaches graduate and undergraduate courses and conducts research for the National Reading Research Center. She has been an elementary classroom teacher and reading specialist in schools in the Washington, DC, metropolitan area. She is the coauthor of six books on reading instruction and over 70 articles published in journals such as *Reading Research Quarterly, The Reading Teacher, Journal of Reading, Educational Psychologist*, and *Journal of Educational Research*. Her primary interests are in the areas of reading comprehension strategy instruction, literacy motivation, and the role of discussion in teaching and learning. She recently completed a three-year term as an elected member of the Board of Directors of the International Reading Association and has also served as coeditor of *The Journal of Reading Behavior*. Her most recent research has focused on identifying classroom factors related to literacy motivation.

John T. Guthrie is professor of human development at the University of Maryland, College Park, Maryland, USA, and codirector of the National Reading Research Center (NRRC). The NRRC is a U.S. federally funded consortium of the University of Maryland and the University of Georgia. The Center conducts studies of reading, writing, science and history learning, assessment, and professional development. Prior to this position, Guthrie headed the University of Maryland's Center for Educational Research and Development. Guthrie was director of research for the International Reading Association from 1974 to 1984. He received his Ph.D. in educational psychology from the University of Illinois. He has published more than 100 articles and edited professional books. In 1992 the National Reading Conference honored him with the Oscar Causey Award for Outstanding Contributions to Reading Research. He is a fellow in the American Psychological Association, American Psychological Society, the National Council of Research in English, and was elected to the Reading Hall of Fame in 1994. His interests are literacy development and environments for learning.

Douglas K. Hartman is an associate professor in the language and literacy program at the University of Pittsburgh, Pittsburgh, Pennsylvania, USA. He started his career by teaching elementary, middle, and high school students in California and Oregon. He later earned his master's degree in reading from California State University, Fresno, and his Ph.D. in literacy and language from the University of Illinois at Urbana-Champaign. He currently teaches preservice and graduate courses on reading and language arts. While his research has received a number of awards from the scholarly community, Hartman's focus has been on the practical matters of how to help students become better integrators and synthesizers of information as they read and write their way across multiple texts.

Dorothy J. Leal has taught children from kindergarten through sixth grade for over 15 years, both in the United States and abroad. She is presently an assistant professor of graduate and undergraduate courses in reading, language arts, children's literature, process writing, and gifted education at Ohio University, Athens, Ohio, USA. She is coauthor with Turnbull, Turnbull, and Shank of the 1995 textbook *Exceptional Lives: Special Education in Today's Schools* (Prentice Hall).

Maureen Lewis was a research fellow on the Exeter Extending Literacy (EXEL) Project at the University of Exeter School of Education in Exeter, England, and is now a lecturer in education at the University of Plymouth, Plymouth, England. She has published widely in a variety of professional and research journals, particularly on the topic of children reading and writing nonfiction texts effectively.

Jane Brady Matanzo is a professor at Florida Atlantic University, Boca Raton and Port St. Lucie, Florida, USA, where she teaches reading, language arts, and children's literature courses. She received her doctorate from the University of Maryland and other degrees from Ohio State University and Ball State University. Her past work has included school administrative and teaching posts, director of graduate reading, and director of teacher education. Her research interests include multicultural education, teachers as researchers, and integration of the language arts. She has coauthored two books: *Raising Readers, Sharing Literature with Young Children* (Walker) and *Programmed Reading Diagnosis for Teachers with Prescriptive References* (Charles Merrill).

Susan Anders Mazzoni is a doctoral fellow in the Department of Curriculum and Instruction at the University of Maryland, College Park, Maryland, USA, where she is studying reading education. She is also a research assistant at the National Reading Research Center where she has worked on the literacy motivation project. Her work has been published in the *Honors College Review* and *The Reading Teacher*. Mazzoni has teaching experience in Baltimore County and Baltimore City public schools and has been teaching adults to read at the Learning Bank of Baltimore since 1988. She earned her undergraduate degree at the University of Maryland, Baltimore County, where she studied philosophy and education and received the Outstanding Senior Award in both departments. Mazzoni is a member of the International Reading Association and Phi Delta Kappa. Her research interests are in the area of discussion and reading motivation.

Ann D. McCann is a graduate research assistant at the National Reading Research Center. She is currently pursuing a M.Ed. and elementary teaching certificate in the Department of Curriculum and Instruction at the University of Maryland, College Park, Maryland, USA. Her research interests include designing and evaluating learning contexts that foster literacy engagement through interdisciplinary teaching.

Lea M. McGee is an associate professor of education at Boston College, Chestnut Hill, Massachusetts, USA. Her current research interests are in exploring young children's responses to literature and the use of multicultural literature in the classroom. She is coauthor of *Literacy's Beginnings: Supporting Young Readers and Writers* (Allyn & Bacon) and *Teaching Reading with Literature: Case Studies to Action Plans* (Merrill-Macmillan). She has published in several professional journals including *Reading Research Quarterly, Journal of Reading Behavior, The Reading Teacher*, and *Language Arts*.

Susan I. McMahon is an assistant professor at the University of Wisconsin, Madison, Wisconsin, USA. After sixteen years of teaching in elementary and secondary classrooms in both public and private schools, she returned to graduate school to pursue an interest in early literacy acquisition. She is interested in literacy processes and tries to model her own teaching through methods supported in recent theory, research, and practice.

Lesley Mandel Morrow is a professor and coordinator of the early childhood education graduate programs at Rutgers University's Graduate School of Education, New Brunswick, New Jersey, USA. She has published extensively in professional journals and edited or authored several books, including the third edition of *Literacy Development in the Early Years: Helping Children Read and Write* (Allyn & Bacon). She has received grants and awards for her research dealing with early literacy development with children from diverse backgrounds, and received the Interntional Reading Association's Outstanding Teacher Educator in Reading Award in 1994. She is a principal research investigator for the National Reading Research Center, and was elected to the Board of Directors of the International Reading Association for 1996 to 1999.

Alfredo Schifini has been a secondary teacher, an elementary reading specialist, and school administrator. He is currently a professor of curriculum and instruction at California State University, Los Angeles, California, USA. Prior to his academic appointment, he was responsible for language arts instruction for the 85 school districts in Los Angeles County. In 1994 he contributed to the International Reading Association monograph, *Kids Come in All Languages*. Schifini has trained K–12 teachers in language and literacy development in bilingual and multilingual settings, and content instruction for second language learners. He has served as the national curriculum consultant to the Guatemalan and Nicaraguan Ministries of Education and was a Fulbright Scholar. He was the recipient of the UCLA award for outstanding achievement in doctoral studies.

Kelly A. Sherrill recently graduated magna cum laude with a bachelor's degree in elementary education from the University of Georgia. She has been a student teacher in both the fourth and second grades. She founded the University of Georgia's Chapter of Student Professional Association of Georgia Educators, serves as an officer in Kappa Delta Epsilon, and received outstanding leadership awards in both Kappa Delta Epsilon and Kappa Delta Pi. She is presently pursuing her master's degree at the University of Georgia, Athens, Georgia, USA.

MaryEllen Vogt is an associate professor of education at California State University, Long Beach, California, USA, where she teaches courses in reading/language arts methods. For 15 years, she served as a classroom teacher, special education teacher, reading specialist, district resource teacher, and curriculum director. She received her doctorate in language and literacy from the University of California, Berkeley. Vogt is a past president of the California Reading Association and was elected to the Board of Directors of the International Reading Association for 1993 to 1996. In 1994 she received the Marcus Foster Memorial Award for outstanding contributions to the field of reading from the California Reading Association. She has served as a consultant in reading/language arts for school districts and reading associations throughout the country, as well as in Canada, Argentina, and Hungary.

Barbara J. Walker was elected to the Board of Directors of the International Reading Association for 1994 to 1997. She is professor and chair of the Department of Special Education and Reading at Montana State University, Billings, Montana, USA. Walker teaches courses in reading difficulties and works in the reading clinic at her university. Her publications include *Diagnostic Teaching of Reading: Techniques for Instruction and Assessment* (Merrill/Prentice Hall) and *Supporting Struggling Readers* (Pippin). She was a distinguished finalist for the International Reading Association's 1991 Albert J. Harris Award for research in reading disabilities. She is a past local and state president of Montana reading councils as well as a frequent presenter at state, regional, and national literacy conferences.

B. Joyce Wiencek is an assistant professor of reading and language arts at Oakland University in Rochester, Michigan, USA, where she teaches undergraduate and graduate courses. She is interested in students' literacy in elementary and early childhood settings, and social constructivist approaches to teaching and learning. Her doctorate is from the University of Maryland in language and literacy. She received her master's degree in reading from George Mason University, and her Bachelor of Arts in early childhood education from Frostburg State College. Wiencek worked as the elementary supervisor of language arts for the Department of Education in the Commonwealth of Virginia for several years. She has 13 years of public school teaching experience in the primary grades in Maryland and Virginia.

David Wray is senior lecturer in education at the University of Exeter in Exeter, England. He has researched and published extensively in the area of literacy development, having authored or edited over 20 books. He is currently editor of the journal, *Reading*, and was president of the United Kingdom Reading Association for 1992–93. He is the director of the Exeter Extending Literacy (EXEL) Project.

Kimberly Wuenker graduated from the University of Georgia with a bachelor's degree in elementary education. She was a campus leader throughout her four years at the university and was a founding member and two-year president of the University of Georgia Chapter of Reading is Fundamental (RIF-UGA). Winner of numerous awards for leadership at the university, she was also a member of Kappa Delta Epsilon and Omicron Delta Kappa. She is currently pursuing her master's degree in education of the gifted at University of Georgia, Athens, Georgia, USA.

PREFACE

A major goal of this book is to emphasize that it is through the personal *interpretation* of both narrative and informational text that learners come to better understand themselves, others, and the world in which we live, and it is through the *comprehension* of both narrative and informational text that learners build a knowledge base about our world. The contributors to this volume, many of whom are affiliated with the National Reading Research Center, have been conducting classroom-based research and program innovations that focus on helping students develop discussion skills that permit them to explore the world of literature and literacy within an environment that is supportive and tolerant. Thus, the following chapters will provide practical, classroom-based strategies and techniques for using discussion in primary and elementary classrooms to promote interpretation and comprehension of both narrative and informational text.

The volume is organized into four parts: Creating Classroom Cultures That Foster Discussion, Discussion in Action, Creating the Climate: The Role of the Teacher, and Perspectives on Assessing Discussion.

PART I: CREATING CLASSROOM CULTURES THAT FOSTER DISCUSSION

In this introductory section the authors explore the core elements to consider when preparing an elementary classroom for discussion. Janice Almasi's chapter provides definitions of recitations and compares her definitions with the new view of discussion that is the foundational basis of the entire volume. Her chapter also provides authentic examples that illustrate the cognitive, social, and affective benefits of discussions. In Chapter 2, Linda Gambrell provides an overview of the rationale for the resurgence of interest in the role of discussion in elementary classrooms and summarizes what research reveals about discussions.

The ability to take into account the specific cultural needs of diverse learners is central to the creation of a classroom that fosters discussion. In Chapter 3, Alfredo Shifini provides insightful commentary specifically related to multicultural and multilingual considerations for discussions. Additionally, throughout the text authors have woven multicultural issues and issues related to diverse learners (such as students receiving special education services, students acquiring English, and students with diverse language development) throughout their suggestions and examples.

Part II: Discussion in Action

The second section provides readers with an unprecedented look at how discussion might be altered for emergent readers as well as for upper level elementary students. Shelby Barrentine's chapter begins this section with an exciting look at how teachers can use interactive read-alouds to engage young children in discussions before, during, and after the read-aloud event. David Wray and Maureen Lewis then share their ideas from the EXEL project that they have established in the United Kingdom. Their chapter makes the case that children's talk is more likely to be purposeful and to extend and deepen their learning if it arises from their engagement in authentic inquiry-based activities. As an illustration of this, one case study is presented in which six-year-olds become involved in researching suitable plants for their school garden. In Chapter 6, Michelle Commeyras, Kelly Sherrill, and Kimberly Wuenker explore the value of student-posed questions in their work with second graders. Using their own authentic teaching experiences, the authors explore their successes and failures as they attempt to study the questions their students ask and their discussion of these questions.

The section then gives consideration to discussions that are based on informational texts and content learning. John Guthrie and Ann McCann describe "idea circles," which are discussions or concepts fueled by multiple text sources. These discussions of informational trade books occur within the context of an integrated science/language arts curriculum. The authors describe the benefits of idea circles and how educators can create them within their own classrooms. In Chapter 8, Douglas Hartman and Jeanette Allison present a compelling case for making inquiry-oriented discussions a more integral part of classroom practice. Suggestions are provided for getting started with inquiry-oriented discussions in which students use multiple texts to make connections and to communicate information to different audiences for different purposes. Susan Anders Mazzoni and Linda Gambrell then provide powerful descriptions of a number of nonquestioning ways to promote discussion of informational texts, ways to integrate text into discussions, and strategies for stimulating discussion of informational texts. Dorothy Leal then concludes this section by explaining how specific types of texts (such as narrative, informational, and informational storybooks) can influence achievement and learning. This is followed by a discussion of teaching tools that are an integral part of grand conversations related to different types of text.

PART III: CREATING THE CLIMATE: THE ROLE OF THE TEACHER

This section provides practical and informative teaching tips for how to design, initiate, implement, and sustain discussions in a variety of classroom settings. In Chapter 11, Trevor Cairney begins with an overview of the value of student talk in classrooms. He also explains the concepts of scaffolding and guided participation as they pertain to the teacher's role in student learning during discussions.

MaryEllen Vogt then presents a rationale for moving away from teacher-centered talk to student response-centered discussions. Specific suggestions for organizing and managing discussion groups are included as well as recommendations for discussion questions and activities that support a response-centered curriculum. Lea McGee's chapter then provides a view of response-centered talk among emergent readers. She describes the nature of interpretation and how young readers' discussions reflect their ability to move beyond the literal level. Joyce Wiencek provides teachers with a model for planning, initiating, implementing, and sustaining a form of literature discussion group known as conversational discussion groups in elementary classrooms. Conversational discussion groups provide teachers with a means of scaffolding students' interactive and interpretive growth. Susan McMahon's chapter on guiding student-led discussion groups concludes the section and describes how students can benefit from leading their own discussions with teacher support. The chapter begins with a description of practices that can impede students' interactions and limit higher level thinking. The chapter then addresses the role of the teacher in guiding student-led discussion groups and how the teacher can provide instructional support for students to conduct their own discussions.

PART IV: PERSPECTIVES ON ASSESSING DISCUSSION

Assessing students' ability to interact with one another and interpret text has often eluded teachers as they explore and try to implement discussions in their classrooms. In Chapter 16, Jane Matanzo presents a variety of strategies that encourage both students and teachers to engage in reflection and assessment. Specific assessment strategies and techniques include videotape portfolios, specification sheets, discussion circles, and pre- and post-discussion debriefings. Lesley Mandel Morrow then examines the use of story retelling as an instructional strategy for engaging young readers in "talking about" what they have listened to or read. Procedures for using story retelling to assess children's interpretation and comprehension are also presented. Barbara Walker concludes this section by presenting a compelling framework for designing classroom discussions that are conversational and instructional in nature. She offers advice for developing and assessing students' strategic thinking behaviors and explains the necessity for developing students' abilities to assess their own literacy.

Linda B. Gambrell and Janice F. Almasi
Coeditors

ACKNOWLEDGEMENTS

We would like to acknowledge the invaluable editorial and technical assistance of Erin M. White and Lauri DiMatteo of the State University of New York at Buffalo, without whose help this volume surely would not have come together.

AUTHOR NOTE

The work reported herein originated as a National Reading Research Project of the University of Georgia and the University of Maryland. It was supported under the Education Research and Development Centers Program (PR/AWARD NO. 117A20007) as administered by the Office of Educational Research and Improvement, U.S. Department of Education. The findings and opinions expressed in this work do not necessarily reflect the position or policies of the National Reading Research Center, the Office of Educational Research and Improvement, or the U.S. Department of Education.

PART I:
CREATING CLASSROOM
CULTURES THAT FOSTER
DISCUSSION

CHAPTER 1

A New View of Discussion

Janice F. Almasi

The view of discussion presented in this volume is radically different from the depiction of traditional postreading "discussions." This chapter will explore more traditional definitions of discussion and contrast them with a new view of discussion—a definition that views discussions as a forum for collaboratively constructing meaning and for sharing responses. Additionally, the chapter will examine theoretical perspectives and research regarding the cognitive, social-emotional, and affective benefits of discussion.

The new view of discussion that is emerging in the professional literature and classrooms across the United States refers to interactive events in which individuals collaboratively construct meaning or consider alternate interpretations of the text in order to arrive at new understandings. *The American Heritage Dictionary* defines discussion as "consideration of a subject by a group; an earnest conversation" (p. 532). Thus, discussion supposes cognitive engagement to the extent that the participants are actively involved in a dialogic conversation with one another rather than passively reciting answers to questions that may not be personally meaningful.

> **" The interpretations of the reader are not static, but continually shaped by transactions between the reader's experiences and the new information acquired from the text. "**

The authors' definition of "literary discussion" is derived from several theoretical orientations. From a literary standpoint, we believe that meaning is derived from the transaction that occurs between the reader, the text, and the context of the literary act (Bleich, 1978; Iser, 1980; Rosenblatt, 1938/1976; 1978). Thus, the interpretations of the reader are not static, but continually shaped by transactions between the reader's experiences and the new information acquired from the text. Under such circumstances the reader's interpretation constantly evolves, and the interpretation that each person brings to a discussion may ultimately be transformed and shaped by the thoughts and ideas of other group members.

Consequently, we also believe that literacy is inseparable from the cultural and social context in which it occurs; thus, sociocultural and sociolinguistic orientations are also pertinent to our view (Bloome & Bailey, 1992; Brown, Collins, & Duguid, 1989; Rogoff, 1990). As "interpretive communities" of students and teachers interact, alternate interpretations and divergent views may be forwarded that also have an impact on a person's interpretation (Fish, 1980). Thus, the interactions among group members involve a reciprocity in which the actions and reactions of individuals are influenced by one another as they interpret the text (Gall & Gall, 1976). These interactions of individuals within a social environment are referred to as "events." Meaning is then viewed as being located within the *event* rather than in an individual's mind (Gee, 1992; Heap, 1992). Thus, literacy is viewed as primarily a social endeavor (Bloome, 1985; Bloome & Green, 1992), and discussion is viewed as a primary component of the literacy process.

Throughout this volume it is this view of discussion, rather than the view of a recitation, which is intended as authors describe interactions between and among teachers and students. One of the most intriguing comparisons between recitations and discussions occurs when teachers consider students' definitions of discussion. As will be demonstrated, when students participate in recitations, their definitions of postreading discussions suggest that they view them as evaluative events in which they perform for their teacher. However, students participating in classroom cultures in which they have experienced authentic discussion, as defined above, tend to define the purpose of discussions differently than students in recitations:

- We have discussions so that if you don't understand the story you might be able to understand it better if you talk about it. (Jimmy, 4th grade)
- Discussions are to tell what *you* think about the story—to explain why you liked the story and why you didn't. (Bridget, 4th grade)

(Almasi, 1993)

These students' definitions suggest a collaborative environment in which the goal of the event is to share viewpoints, provide a rational argument, and work together to come to new understandings about literature.

TRADITIONAL DISCUSSIONS

"We have discussions so the kids who go to the bathroom can know what they missed." (Corrine, 4th grade)

Corrine's view of discussion differs in many ways from that of researchers and teachers. However, her definition reflects her understanding of a phenomenon based upon the classroom culture that has evolved among the teacher and students in the literate community to which she belongs. Because the nature of classroom literature discussions may vary from classroom to classroom, definitions of discussion occurring in elementary classrooms can vary widely as well.

According to Barr and Dreeben (1991), the format for discussing literature that many children have been exposed to in elementary classrooms is characterized by teacher talk and literal questions rather than student involvement and thinking. These notions have been supported in numerous settings, including research conducted in authentic classroom settings (Almasi, 1995; Almasi & Gambrell, 1994) and survey research at the national level (Foertsch, 1992; Langer, Applebee, Mullis, & Foertsch, 1990). The interaction patterns that occur between teachers and students in these traditional discussions are dominated by recurrent sequences of teacher questions and student answers. The questions asked during these interactions generally require students to recall what they already know about the literature they have read. These patterns are evidenced in the example below, taken from a discussion of an Encyclopedia Brown mystery called *The Case of the Crowing Rooster* (Sobol, 1986).

Initiate	Teacher:	What was Encyclopedia Brown doing when Lisa went by on her bicycle?
Respond	Student 10:	He was trimming the hedges.
Evaluate/ Initiate	Teacher:	He was trimming the hedges okay. Where was Lisa going?
Respond	Student 36:	The city dump.
Evaluate	Teacher:	Okay. Why was she going to the city dump?
		(Almasi, 1993, Transcript #08-40, December 2, 1992)

Cazden (1986) and Mehan (1979) have referred to the type of interaction depicted above as the I-R-E (Initiate-Respond-Evaluate) participatory structure. In such interactions the teacher initiates a topic by asking a question. In this example, the teacher initiated the discussion by asking a question about what Encyclopedia Brown was doing. Students then responded to the question with an answer: "He was trimming the hedges." The teacher followed by evaluating the student's response. In this case, the teacher responded, "Okay, he was trimming the hedges" which indicates to the students that the response that was given was satisfactory. Within the same turn, the teacher then initiates the sequence again by asking another question. Traditional discussions consist of repetitive chains of this nature providing little opportunity for students to interact with one another. In fact, Almasi (1995) reported that, during episodes of sociocognitive conflict, 85% of such teacher-led discussions were sustained by sequences of I-R-E-like discourse. Additionally, these discussions were dominated by the teacher who was responsible for asking 93% of the questions and for talking 62% of the time.

The type of interaction described above is more appropriately called "recitation" rather than discussion because there is no collaborative attempt to construct meaning; the answers are already known. Students merely recite the answers (Dillon, 1984; Gall & Gall, 1976). As such, the literature that is being discussed is treated as *content* with particular answers that are right and wrong rather than as a *literary work* that must be interpreted (Langer, 1992). Therefore, through the remainder of the chapter the more traditional "discussions" described above will be referred to as "recitations."

> **" *In a discussion, the thoughts, ideas, feelings, and responses of all participants contribute to the event.* "**

Students involved in recitations may come to view the purpose of these interactions as primarily for the teacher's sake or for assessment purposes, rather than for constructing meaning. This notion is evidenced in their explanations of why children talk about stories after they read them in school:

- So that you can answer questions when the teacher asks you them.
  (Kristin, 4th grade)
- So that the teacher can see if you were paying attention or not.
  (Ben, 4th grade)
- So that the teacher knows that we really understand what we read, and so he knows when we can change books or move up or down a level.
  (Alicia, 4th grade)
- So the teacher can know what you're thinking in your mind—he has a little piece of what you think.
  (Greg, 4th grade)
- To see if we know a lot and so that when we do our seatwork we can answer the questions.
  (Laura, 4th grade)

(Almasi, 1993)

COMPARING RECITATIONS AND DISCUSSIONS

Perhaps one of the most profound differences between recitations and discussions lies in the perception of *where* meaning resides. In a discussion, the thoughts, ideas, feelings, and responses of all participants who have read a given text contribute to the event and that event has an influence on a participant's eventual interpretation. Figure 1

Figure 1
A transactional view of discussion: Meaning resides within the event.

depicts the type of transaction that occurs in a discussion. A participant is in transaction with the text or texts he or she has read. As participants gather in social context to exchange thoughts, new understandings and meanings may emerge as participants interact with one another. Thus, as noted above, meaning resides in the event.

In contrast, in a recitation there is little interaction among students, so the teacher is the member of the group whose thoughts might influence a person's interpretation most significantly. The fact that the teacher determines the questions that will be asked, the order of those questions, and the correctness of students' responses to those questions means that the teacher becomes the ultimate interpretive authority in the discussion context. Students will tend to shape the nature of their responses to meet their perceptions of what the teacher wants or to construct an interpretation favored by the teacher. Meaning is then viewed as being located within the text and can be extracted or realized by students through teacher questioning.

Any comparison of recitations and discussions must also take into account the social structures that occur in each context and the rules that govern interaction. The teacher's roles as well as the students' roles provide insight into how these social structures compare within each context (see Figures 2 and 3).

> **❝ *In a discussion, students tend to assume a multitude of roles that are traditionally reserved for the teacher, such as inquisitor, facilitator, and evaluator as well as the more familiar role of respondent.* ❞**

STUDENT ROLES

Students tend to participate differently in discussions than in recitations. In a discussion, students tend to assume a multitude of roles that are traditionally reserved for the teacher, such as inquisitor, facilitator, and evaluator as well as the more familiar role of respondent (see Figure 2).

INQUISITOR. As inquisitor, students ask questions that are personally meaningful because the questions will help them interpret and make sense of the text. In support of this, Almasi (1995) and Almasi and Gambrell (1994) found that most of the questions that are asked in discussions are asked by students (84%) and an overwhelming amount of the discourse (94%) is also contributed by students (Almasi, 1995). From this, we learn that two roles that students often assume in discussions are inquisitor and respondent; they are not only asking questions, but are also engaged in substantive dialogue with one another in their efforts to resolve interpretive issues and make sense of the text. The excerpt below, taken from a fourth grade discussion of *Soup's New Shoes* (Peck, 1986) illustrates how students interact with one another, fluidly assuming roles of inquisitor and respondent throughout the discussion of why the main character, Soup, swapped his new shoes with his friend, Rob, who had ripped his old pair:

Inquisitor   Student 102:   I was wondering why Soup gave his shoes, because if I ever gave my shoes to someone else to wear, my Mom would kill me.

Figure 2
Student roles: Recitations vs. discussions.

Recitations	Discussions
Inquisitor: • Students ask few questions	*Inquisitor:* • Students ask questions in order to understand text better and to help construct meaning
Facilitator of Interaction: • Students are called on by the teacher in order to participate and to maintain topic coherence	*Facilitator of Interaction:* • Students encourage each other to participate • Students are responsible for ensuring that all group members stick to the topic • Students are responsible for ensuring that all group members take turns
Facilitator of Interpretation: • Students do not determine the interpretive strategies that are used during the discussion	*Facilitator of Interpretation:* • Students restate or try to question what others have said if it is not clear • Students may relate topic or issue to their own experiences in order to assist understanding • Students may compare/contrast characters • Students may discuss author's style and craft
Respondent: • Students respond to the teacher's questions	*Respondent:* • Students respond to each other's questions
Evaluator: • Students' responses are evaluated by the teacher	*Evaluator:* • Students try to challenge each other's ideas by telling whether they agree or disagree and by telling why

Respondent	Student 43:	[He] probably just [gave his friend his shoes] for the school day and then they traded back.
Respondent	Student 69:	Probably since like he might have something to do that night [and needed] like a good pair of shoes to wear.
Respondent	Student 48:	When they traded shoes Soup asked, "How does your shoe fit?" and Rob said, "Your shoes are a little bit big for me. How are mine, how do mine feel?" "Well," said Soup, "one is awfully tight and one is awfully loose."

Respondent	Student 43:	He [Soup] gave him the shoes so he would stop crying, but they'll probably trade back at the end of the day.
Respondent	Student 71:	But they might not trade back.
Respondent	Student 102:	I bet they will. You traded shoes!
Respondent	Student 48:	But his Mom would be very upset.
Inquisitor	Student 71:	If you paid for your own shoes, would your Mom be upset if you ripped 'em?
Respondent	Student 48:	No.
Respondent	Student 102:	If you paid for 'em, you can do whatever you want with 'em.
Respondent	Student 8:	I think Soup's Mom would not be upset, because it doesn't tell you in the story.
Respondent	Student 69:	It doesn't tell you anything about his Mom in the story.

(Almasi, 1993, Transcript #08-41, December 2, 1992)

Notice in this example that the pattern of interaction among students differs from the I-R-E pattern that typified recitations. After a question, rather than one response followed by an evaluation, students offered several responses to the inquiry. The discussion is focused because students' responses are relevant to the topic and they are able to share their thoughts and ideas and relate to their own personal experiences.

FACILITATOR. Students also begin to facilitate their own interactions by encouraging group members to actively participate once teachers relinquish the responsibility to them. In the following example, student 65 demonstrates this as the students are discussing *McBroom Tells the Truth* (Fleischman, 1989). Knowing that many of the other group members have often dominated aspects of the discussion, and knowing that student 71 was relatively passive, student 65 encourages him to join in the discussion:

Student 102:	I liked the story because it was a nice story to read, and it tells how he [McBroom] was almost cheated out of his nice farm, but when he found out what a rich top soil it had, and all the things he planted grew in a few hours he...
Student 94:	I like this story because I have a book like this story, and it's kinda like people living on the farm and buying land from someone else.
Student 65:	71, what do you think about the story?
Student 71:	I think it's good. I like it.
Student 65:	Would you tell it to a friend?

Student 102: I think it was a nice story, and I would share it with my friend or someone because it was a funny story, and it had lots of things happening in it and...

Student 48: As I read the story I liked it, and then when I got on the bus I told my friend about it, and they thought it is a good story because it is about the western, and it is about some of the old times and took place when there were pioneers.

Student 8: This story reminded me of when we grew a lot of vegetables in our backyard.

(Almasi, 1993, Transcript #03-41, October 14, 1992)

In this example we see how student 65 effectively took on a new role to foster interaction among his peers and to encourage the quieter student (71) to join the discussion. After receiving a very limited, but affirmative response from student 71, we see how student 65 encouraged further participation by asking whether he would tell it to a friend. Although student 71 yielded to the more dominant student 102, he may not have joined in the discussion at all had student 65 not assumed the role of facilitator and encouraged his participation. Throughout the ensuing weeks student 71's classmates continued to encourage him to participate, and after the first semester he was actively participating by asking thought provoking questions and making insightful responses.

EVALUATOR. Another role that students often assume is evaluator. In this role, however, students do not necessarily assess the accuracy of their peers' comments, but offer alternative or divergent viewpoints. In the following example, these fourth grade students have read Levy's *Something Strange at the Ballpark* (1986). They are sharing their opinions about the story as well as how they might improve it:

Student 48: I like the story because I like baseball.

Student 71: I liked the story because it's a mystery.

Student 65: I like the characters, and I wish instead of the baseball bat got stolen, I wanted the glove to get stolen.

Student 69: I know, rather than the baseball bat, but I'd rather the glove [interruptions from other members] the glove, I mean the baseball bat, because you can't play without a glove, you can play without a baseball bat because you can just borrow someone else's.

Student 94: I wish nothing got stolen because it's not nice to steal other things.

Student 102: But it's a mystery so they have to steal something.

All: [nod heads affirmatively in agreement]

(from Almasi, 1993, Transcript #05-41, October 28, 1992)

After hearing student 94's comment, "I wish nothing got stolen because it's not nice to steal other things," student 102 assumes the role of evaluator in that he rejects the comment based upon what he knows about the mystery genre. His reminder captures the attention and approval of the other group members. Examples such as this suggest that not every response is accepted in a discussion. If members are listening intently and truly attempting to collaboratively come to new understanding, some responses further the group's progress, and others may not. In this case, student 94's comment was not denounced, but became less acceptable in light of what the students brought into the discussion based upon their knowledge of mysteries. Such conflicts promote critical and evaluative thinking that differs from the passive role that students assume during recitation as they await the evaluative commentary of their teachers. As we have seen in these brief examples, when given the opportunity to assume roles typically reserved for teachers, students readily adopt them into their own repertoire.

In the new view of discussion presented in this text, students clearly play a much more active role in the meaning construction process. As inquisitors they negotiate the topics for discussion that are of interest and concern to them, as respondents they are actively involved in reacting to the thoughts of their peers, as facilitators they steer the discussion and maintain responsibility for their actions, and as evaluators they demonstrate their ability to listen and to think critically about their peers' comments.

TEACHERS' ROLES

The teacher's role in a discussion also shifts in comparison to his or her role in a recitation (see Figure 3). In a discussion teachers act more as facilitators, scaffolding student interaction and interpretation when needed. In the following example, taken from a fourth grade discussion of *If You Say So, Claude* (Nixon, 1989), we see how the teacher scaffolds students' interpretations by encouraging them to provide a rationale for their response. Likewise, by encouraging students to share whether they agree or disagree with others' comments, the teacher also encourages students to assume the role of evaluator within the discussion:

Student 41: At the end of the story it says, "She gave Claude the biggest smile he'd ever seen anyone come up with, " and she said, "If you say so Claude." I like that part at the end of the story.

Student 54: I liked the part right here. It says, "Shirley's aim was never good, so she missed the rabbit. The old bullet bounced off the rock and back and forth across the canyon, whanging and banging, and zinging and zanging, making a terrible racket. Shirley and the rabbit just froze, staring wide-eyed at each other."

Teacher: Okay, I noticed one thing is we're doing a very good job of people finding parts that they like and giving their opinion. But I don't get to hear why we liked it, or if someone else agrees or disagrees. Also, what does that part mean to you? Okay? Let's develop these topics a little bit.

The discourse that immediately follows the teacher's scaffolding shows the students' initial attempts to improve their discussion:

Student 93: Um, on the that one page where I said where that wild hog was, it um, at first I didn't know what she was holding onto. And then when I read more it said the snake wrapped around it and it was squeezing it to death.

Student 54: I agree, I agree because the snake—it didn't look like a snake.

Student 93: I know. It didn't really look like a snake.

Student 45: It looked like she was just holding it with her palm of. . .

Student 54: . . .hand, like that [demonstrates].

Student 93: Uh huh [nods affirmatively].

Student 54: You could tell, but when you got closer to it you could see the tongue and the head.

Student 45: Yeah, uh huh. I agree because the head, like the snake's tongue's hanging out, and she's squeezing the snake and holding it, the hog, the wild hog, at the same time.

(Almasi, 1993, Transcript #03-11, October 14, 1992)

As a facilitator of the interaction and interpretation, the teacher fosters discussion that is more focused around a central topic; the discussion begins to lead children to richer understandings and interpretations.

One of the traditional roles reserved for teachers in a recitation is the evaluation of students' responses. This role is necessary if one subscribes to the notion that there is one correct interpretation that can be found in a text. However, in the new view of discussion, where meaning is located in the event and that meaning may be different to different individuals, teachers are not in pursuit of evaluating the *adequacy* of students' knowledge (Orsolini & Pontecorvo, 1992), or the *content* of a reader's memory as it compares to one literal meaning of the text (Pressley, et al., 1992).

In order to evaluate students' success in a discussion, teachers must consider the question: What must students do in a discussion to show that they are knowledgeable? Typically, we have assumed that comprehension was the primary indicator of a student's knowledge. During recitations, such knowledge is often demonstrated by stu-

Figure 3
Teacher roles: Recitations vs. discussions.

Recitations	Discussions
Inquisitor: • Teacher asks most of the questions • Teacher's questions are usually pre-determined and are text-based in nature	*Inquisitor:* • Teacher asks few questions • Teachers may occasionally model good questioning for students by asking an open-ended question that encourages student participation
Facilitator of Interaction: • Teacher coordinates/determines who responds to questions • Most of the interaction and discourse flows through the teacher	*Facilitator of Interaction* • Teacher encourages as much interaction as possible among students • Interaction does not flow through teacher
Facilitator of Interpretation: • Teacher's questions often lead students to a single interpretation of text • Teacher often offers insight into own interpretation of text	*Facilitator of Interpretation:* • Teacher remains neutral on interpretational issues
Respondent: • Teacher usually does at least 50% of the talking	*Respondent:* • Teacher remains silent as much as possible
Evaluator: • Teacher gives feedback as to the correctness of students' responses almost immediately through either verbal or nonverbal means	*Evaluator:* • Teacher exploits only the best opportunities to give feedback on interaction or interpretational issues

dents as they respond to teacher-initiated questions that tend to be literal in nature (Gall, 1984). Retellings of story events have also been suggested as an assessment task for measuring comprehension (Johnston, 1983; Mandler & Johnson, 1977; Stein & Glenn, 1979) and have been shown to enhance recall and comprehension of text (Gambrell, Pfeiffer, & Wilson, 1985).

Knowledgeable students in such interactions can accurately recall and retell textual information. Both of these methods of determining knowledge focus on assessing an end *product*. This view of knowledge implies that there is a solitary interpretation inherent to the text that can be extracted and verbalized by students. It is assumed that such verbalization during a discussion displays a student's understanding or comprehension of the text. However, such practice denies the importance of the social context in the evolution of a person's understanding (Carlsen, 1991), and not only suggests that there is a single, correct meaning to the text, but that the reader's understanding is complete upon entering a discussion (Langer, 1992).

Our understanding of what illustrates students' knowledge during discussions focuses on the *process* by which they come to an understanding or an interpretation of text. This view recognizes and celebrates the role of culture and society in shaping a student's evolving interpretations during the literary transaction. Thus, the learning that occurs and the knowledge that is displayed within discussions of literature cannot be examined without taking the activity, context, and classroom culture into account (Brown, Collins, & Duguid, 1989). The knowledge that students display may be evident in their ability to demonstrate communicative competence in their interactions with others (Bloome & Bailey, 1992). This may mean that students display their ability to initiate topics of conversation, link information that they want to communicate to what has already been discussed, respond to the comments of others, and speak in a manner that enables them to be understood by others.

Knowledge may also be displayed in terms of a student's interpretive abilities. We may need to look at the process by which a group constructs meaning and look at what interpretive abilities a student is able to exhibit in a particular circumstance. Such knowledge may involve an ability to compare characters, make intertextual connections to other books, challenge the author's style of writing, or critically examine the text from more than one perspective.

The teacher's role as evaluator during discussions moves from assessing the correctness of students' responses to evaluating the process by which students construct meaning. Similarly, teachers act more as facilitators who scaffold students' attempts as they learn to interact meaningfully and thoughtfully about text.

BENEFITS OF DISCUSSION

Vygotsky (1978) theorized that social environments provide learners with the opportunity to observe higher levels of cognitive processing. From this perspective, discussions of literature may be viewed as a social environment in which students can witness how group members work together to collaboratively construct meaning while also participating in the process.

Learning, in this situation, may occur incidentally as the learner observes the cognitive processes of fellow group members as they develop an interpretation.

Learning may also be more direct when teachers or peers function as more knowledgeable participants and scaffold the interaction so that the learner becomes capable of achieving more with their assistance than they could have independently (Rogoff, 1990; Vygotsky, 1978).

The benefits of participating in classroom discussions of literature are numerous. From a cognitive standpoint, students may gradually internalize some of the interpretive behaviors that are associated with higher levels of thinking. From a social perspective, students may develop better competence during social interactions. Participation may also elicit affective benefits as students begin to enjoy reading literature. Thus, the values of engaging students in discussion are numerous and center around cognitive, social, and affective dimensions.

> **" Discussions of literature may be viewed as a social environment in which students can witness how group members work together to collaboratively construct meaning. "**

COGNITIVE BENEFITS OF ENGAGING IN DISCUSSION

Student 71: I wonder why um Soup said in the shoe store the guy had an X-ray machine?

Student 102: I don't know why 'cuz why would a shoe salesman buy that kind of equipment just to sell shoes?

Student 43: They usually have just the foot measuring thing. You take off your shoes and stick your foot on it.

Student 48: Not a machine. They didn't have them back then.

Student 69: An X-ray machine—he's probably like a doctor and a shoe salesman in one.

Student 71: That's what I thought.

(overtalk)

Student 71: He [the main character] said it was for to see if the foot fit the shoe.

Student 48: Like how big your bones are, and how much you had to grow.

Student 102: If you want to see your skin on an X-ray machine—what's an X-ray machine for?

Student 48: That's true.

Student 43: Because just to see if the foot could fit in the shoe. Because your skin's gonna be over the bone when it goes into the shoe.

Student 102: Well actually the X-ray machine is just so you can see how big your foot really is. The skin will just cover it up.

(Almasi, 1993, Transcript #08-41, December 2, 1992)

Participation in collaborative discussions provides students with a number of cognitive benefits that are illustrated in this example from a fourth grade group discussion of *Soup's New Shoes*. Students are naturally inquisitive, and when afforded the opportunity to verbalize their wonderings about text, as student 71 does in this example, students exhibit their ability to monitor their understanding.

When students ask questions such as the ones in the example, it is generally because they are attempting to arrive at an interpretation of the text. In this instance the students could not understand why a shoe salesman would need to have an X-ray machine. Thus, they were experiencing a conflict between their understanding of the modern uses of X-ray machines and the use suggested in the text. Given that the setting for the story was in the 1930s it may be that students were having difficulty relating to the use of a medical tool for another purpose.

From a cognitive perspective, when students are encouraged to verbalize these conflicts they learn how to raise uncertainties in their understandings, explain and justify their positions, seek information to help them resolve the uncertainty, and learn to see alternative points of view (Almasi, 1995; Brown & Palincsar, 1989; Doise & Mugny, 1984; Johnson & Johnson, 1979; Mugny & Doise, 1978; Webb & Palincsar, in press).

Another cognitive benefit is that students can learn from one another in their interactions. In a collaborative discussion, one student can assist another student who may have an uncertainty. Thus, peers can function as tutors for one another as they learn how to interpret text. In the example below we see student 13 raising an uncertainty about the dog's action in the story *Something Strange at the Ballpark*.

Student 13: Why did the dog jump up when someone pulled his tail?

Student 52: Because…

Student 89: Because someone pulled his tail.

Student 52: Nuh uh. He smelled the scent. He smelled the scent of the glove so he ran after Marshall.

Student 13: [reading from text] "He jumped up as if someone had pulled his tail." Nobody pulled his tail. He jumped up *as if* someone had pulled his tail, but no one pulled his tail.

Student 89: It says right here, "Jill tied it [invisible string] to Fletcher's tail." The baseball glove was a trap. Jill tied it to Fletcher's tail [with invisible string].

Student 13:   Detective kit

Student 52:   Oh yeah! I get it!

Student 89:   Right there. Look. Read it.

Student 52:   See look it's...it's...it says, "Jill tied it to Fletcher's tail. She..."

Student 89:   "...used invisible string from my detective kit."

(Almasi, 1993, Transcript #05-61, October 28, 1992)

In this example we see students working through the "zone of proximal development" (Vygotsky, 1978) as they take turns instructing one another. Initially student 13 functioned in the role of learner and students 89 and 52 as tutors as they shared their thoughts. Unsatisfied with this information, student 13 then enacted a cognitive strategy whereby she sought information from the text to help her resolve her conflict. The information that she found was enough to convince the other students to alter their interpretations. Over time student 13's enactment of the cognitive strategy of referring to the text to resolve uncertainty may gradually be internalized by other group members who may use it at other points to resolve their own uncertainties or those raised by other group members. Thus, when students are provided with the opportunity to interact with one another they are exposed to a variety of higher cognitive functions that enable them to gradually internalize such functions (Almasi, 1995; Almasi & Gambrell, 1994).

When students share their thoughts with others their thoughts become an object that can be reflected upon. By sharing, these thoughts are made available to all group members for inspection and provide an opportunity to expand a student's limited perceptions. Thus, student interaction in discussions may be an important factor in promoting the ability to think critically and to consider multiple perspectives (Prawat, 1989) and in developing the ability to confirm, extend, and modify their individual interpretations of texts (Eeds & Wells, 1989; Leal, 1992).

Also evident in the examples above is that when students are given autonomy to explore their own topics for discussions of literature, the quality of their discourse is enhanced. Students who participate in discussions of text not only engage in more dialogue about text, but the quality of their discourse is more complex than the dialogue of studnts who participate in more traditional teacher-led recitations (Almasi, 1995; Almasi & Gambrell, 1994; Eeds & Wells, 1989; Leal, 1992; Sweigart, 1991). Additionally, when teachers provided greater opportunities for students to share their opinions about a text, the types of responses that students

" Peers can function as tutors for one another as they learn how to interpret text. "

share broaden (Martinez, Roser, Hoffman, & Battle, 1992) and reflect their personal reactions to the text (McGee, 1992).

SOCIAL-EMOTIONAL BENEFITS OF ENGAGING IN DISCUSSION

During discussions of literature the focus is on the process by which interpretations are constructed through interaction and the negotiation of meaning within the social context of the classroom. Students learn to become literate by being involved in the types of processes that are central to the social transmission of knowledge in a given society (Cook-Gumperz, 1986). Part of the discussion culture involves the participatory roles that individuals assume within the group. Students and teachers tend to assume static roles during interactions characterized as "recitations" (Baxter, 1988). Teachers assume the role of inquisitor and evaluator, and students assume the role of respondent. In classroom discussions of literature that feature extensive dialogue and interaction, students assume a variety of roles and are able to assume roles that are typically reserved for the teacher (McMahon 1992; O'Flahavan; 1989).

Within classroom discussions, the responsibility for learning is transferred from teacher to students. In such an environment students come to believe that they can control their own learning as they learn how to interact with one another (Alvermann, O'Brien, & Dillon, 1990; O'Flahavan, 1989; Slavin, 1990). The example below displays how the teacher functions as a scaffold in terms of teaching students strategies for interacting more effectively. The teacher demonstrates that the students have shifted topics several times without exploring any of the issues in detail. This type of behavior lets students know that they are not maintaining a topic of conversation and also reminds them to avoid topic changes.

Student 54: One of my questions is why is the black stallion so rough?

Student 61: One of my questions is why does he ride every year?

Student 46: I think that Grandpa was brave to ride Rolling Thunder and strong to keep holding the...

Teacher: Before you go on let me just throw something out to you. We just had one person ask a question, another person ask a question, and another person give a comment. We have three different things going on, and we didn't finish any of them. Let's just take one at a time, finish it, and then go on.

Student 41: I wouldn't want to ride Rolling Thunder because he's too rough, and even if people would give me $500 I would not ride him. I would not want to get launched from a horse.

Student 54: The black stallion is so rough because he's wild, and he's not used to being tame.

Student 57:   He's not used to being *rode*.

Student 61:   [to Student 54] You're changing the subject.

> (Almasi, 1993, Transcript #02-11, October 7, 1992)

Within a span of a few minutes the teacher's suggestion was acted upon by the students. In this case, student 61 assumed responsibility for monitoring the group's ability to maintain topics and pointed out to student 54 that he had changed the subject away from the question of why Grandfather rides the horse every year, back to the earlier unresolved topic of why the horse was so rough. Thus, students involved in discussions not only learn how to interact socially and develop communicative competence, but they learn to take responsibility for their own learning.

"Students involved in discussions not only learn how to interact socially and develop communicative competence, but they learn to take responsibility for their own learning."

From another perspective, student involvement in discussions has benefits in terms of social-emotional issues related to the way students perceive their own competence, as well as their attitudes toward others. Slavin (1990) reported that student participation in discussions increases self-esteem while fostering positive attitudes and friendships among students of different races or ethnic backgrounds; acceptance of mainstreamed academically handicapped students; positive relationships among classmates; cooperation with others; support from classmates; and the ability to identify others' viewpoints and understand their feelings.

AFFECTIVE BENEFITS OF ENGAGING IN DISCUSSIONS

A recent reanalysis of the National Assessment of Educational Progress database found that social interaction was positively associated with reading activity (Guthrie, Schafer, Wang, & Afflerbach, 1995). In particular, students of all ages who talked with their friends and parents about what they read were more active readers than students who engaged in less discourse about their literate behaviors. This information is consistent with the findings of Morrow and Weinstein (1986) who reported that scope of reading increased when students and teachers participated in discussion and debate about the ideas present in the texts they read.

These findings suggest that students who talk about what they read are more likely to engage in reading. When students have the opportunity to discuss what they read they are also more likely to respond aesthetically by sharing their thoughts and emotions about the text as they read it (Many & Wiseman, 1992). This is evidenced in the excerpt below taken from a fourth grade discussion of *If You Say So, Claude*.

Student 69: I did not like part of the story because there are just two main characters. They didn't really say anything about them or their house. They didn't tell you anything about it at all.

Student 65: See I thought that Shirley was the only main character. I didn't think Claude was a main character.

Students 69: But it keeps on saying, "If you say so Claude."

Student 102: Yes, but Claude was hardly in it, but Shirley was the main...

Student 65: But Shirley was saying it.

Student 71: Did I say that this story reminded me of when I was in Baltimore? They got stuff like this. They got horses and they carried something, but it wasn't called a wagon.

Student 94: It reminded me of when I went to this place close to my house. They had people with hats...I should say bonnets that they wore on their heads.

Student 102: Like Student 69 said, there weren't too many characters. I think they should have added more characters in this story.

Student 94: My favorite character was Claude.

Student 102: I thought that this was a funny story because she [Shirley] did not have good aim, and she was making the bullets fire everywhere and it never hit anything like the bobcat. It hit the tree and things were falling off and tumbling down the hill.

Student 65: Well I think she did not have good aim because she didn't aim.

(Almasi, 1993, Transcript #04-41, October 22, 1992)

In this excerpt students offer their reactions to the characters as well as the author's style of writing when they suggest that perhaps more characters would have improved the story. Additionally, students were able to relate parts of the story to their own experiences.

Students also benefit from discussions because they often make discoveries about themselves as individuals and as learners. Their responses reflect their beliefs and attitudes as well as their learning strategies. In the following example these fourth graders are sharing their reactions to *McBroom Tells the Truth*. The students are sharing their reactions when they

> **" Students who talk about what they read are more likely to engage in reading. "**

first encountered the names of all 11 of McBroom's children as it appeared in the text, "I turned to our children, 'Will*jill*hester*chester*peter*polly*tim*tom*mary*larry*andlittle*clarinda*.'"

Student 102: First [when I saw the name] I am like, "What does this word say?" Then I say all the Will, Jill, and everyone. I was surprised that they had all those kids. I was thinking they might have had some space between the names, but they were all next to each other so I thought it was one name.

Student 94: When I saw it for the first time I skipped it and read the story to the end, and then I came back to that, and I was figuring out what it said.

Student 65: I think that it is weird.

(Almasi, 1993, Transcript #03-41, October 14, 1992)

By sharing their reactions to the unusual text as well as their strategies for handling the text, students revealed their own learning strategies, which may help them come to new understandings about the text and themselves.

As students participate in discussions of literature, there are many opportunities for cognitive, social, emotional, and affective growth. When classroom cultures allow opportunities for authentic discussion, students' perceptions of the literary process, as well as their literary competence, are affected in ways that reflect that culture. Views of discussion as merely an assessment tool for the teacher may give way to views that highlight the importance of talk to the construction of meaningful interpretations of literature.

References

ALMASI, J.F. (1993). *The nature of fourth graders' sociocognitive conflicts in peer-led and teacher-led discussions of literature*. Unpublished doctoral dissertation, University of Maryland, College Park.

ALMASI, J.F. (1995). The nature of fourth graders' sociocognitive conflicts in peer-led and teacher-led discussions of literature. *Reading Research Quarterly, 30*(3), 314–351.

ALMASI, J.F., & GAMBRELL, L.B. (1994). *Sociocognitive conflict in peer-led and teacher-led discussions of literature* (Research Report No. 12). Athens, GA: Universities of Maryland and Georgia, National Reading Research Center.

ALVERMANN, D.E., O'BRIEN, D.G., & DILLON, D.R. (1990). What teachers do when they say they're having discussions of content area reading assignments: A qualitative analysis. *Reading Research Quarterly, 25*(4), 296–322.

THE AMERICAN HERITAGE DICTIONARY (3rd edition, 1992). Boston, MA: Houghton Mifflin.

BARR, R., & DREEBEN, R. (1991). Grouping students for reading instruction. In R. Barr, M.L. Kamil, P.B. Mosenthal, & P.D. Pearson (Eds.), *Handbook of reading research* (Vol. 2, pp. 885–910). White Plains, NY: Longman.

BAXTER, E.P. (1988). Turn-taking in tutorial group discussion under varying conditions of preparation and leadership. *Higher Education, 17,* 295–306.

BLEICH, D. (1978). *Subjective criticism*. Baltimore, MD: Johns Hopkins University Press.

BLOOME, D. (1985). Reading as a social process. *Language Arts, 62*(2), 134–142.

BLOOME, D., & BAILEY, F.M. (1992). Studying language and literacy through events, particularity, and intertextuality. In R. Beach, J.L. Green, M.L. Kamil, & T. Shanahan (Eds.), *Multidisciplinary perspectives on literacy research* (pp. 181–210). Urbana, IL: National Conference on Research in English and the National Council of Teachers of English.

BLOOME, D., & GREEN, J.L. (1992). Educational contexts of literacy. In W.A. Grabe (Ed.), *Annual review of applied linguistics* (Vol. 12, pp. 49–70). New York: Cambridge University Press.

BROWN, A.L., & PALINCSAR, A.S. (1989). Guided, cooperative learning and individual knowledge acquisition. In L.B. Resnick (Ed.), *Knowing, learning, and instruction: Essays in honor of Robert Glaser* (pp. 393–451). Hillsdale, NJ: Erlbaum.

BROWN, J.S., COLLINS, A., & DUGUID, P. (1989). Situated cognition of learning. *Educational Researcher, 18*, 32–42.

CARLSEN, W. (1991). Questioning in classrooms: A sociolinguistic perspective. *Review of Educational Research, 61*(2), 157–178.

CAZDEN, C.B. (1986). Classroom discourse. In M.C. Wittrock (Ed.), *Handbook of research on teaching* (3rd ed., pp. 432–463). New York: Macmillan.

COOK-GUMPERZ, J. (1986). Introduction: The social construction of literacy. In J. Cook-Gumperz (Ed.), *The social construction of literacy* (pp. 1–15). New York: Cambridge University Press.

DILLON, J.T. (1984). Research on questioning and discussion. *Educational Leadership, 42*(3), 50–56.

DOISE, W., & MUGNY, G. (1984). *The social development of the intellect.* Oxford, UK: Pergamon Press.

EEDS, M., & WELLS, D. (1989). Grand conversations: An exploration of meaning construction in literature study groups. *Research in the Teaching of English, 23*(10), 4–29.

FISH, S. (1980). *Is there a text in this class: The authority of interpretive communities.* Cambridge, MA: Harvard University Press.

FOERTSCH, M.A. (1992, May). *Reading in and out of school: Factors influencing the literacy achievement of American students in grades 4, 8, and 12, in 1988 and 1990* (Vol. 2). Washington, DC: National Center for Education Statistics.

GALL, M. (1984). Synthesis of research on teachers' questioning. *Educational Leadership, 42*(3), 40–47.

GALL, M.D., & GALL, J.P. (1976). The discussion method. In N.L. Gage (Ed.), *The psychology of teaching methods* (no. 75, pt. 1, pp. 166–216). Chicago, IL: University of Chicago Press.

GAMBRELL, L.B., PFEIFFER, W.R., & WILSON, R.M. (1985). The effects of retelling upon reading comprehension and recall of text information. *Journal of Educational Research, 78*(4), 216–220.

GEE, J. (1992). Socio-cultural approaches to literacy (literacies). In W.A. Grabe (Ed.), *Annual Review of Applied Linguistics* (Vol. 12, pp. 31–48). New York: Cambridge University Press.

GUTHRIE, J.T., SCHAFER, W.D., WANG, Y.Y., & AFFLERBACH, P.P. (1995). Influences of instruction on reading engagement: An empirical exploration of a social-cognitive framework of reading activity. *Reading Research Quarterly, 30*(1), 8–25.

HEAP, J.L. (1992). Ethnomethodology and the possibility of a metaperspective on literacy research. In R. Beach, J.L. Green, M.L. Kamil, & T. Shanahan (Eds.), *Multidisciplinary perspectives on literacy research* (pp. 35–56). Urbana, IL: National Conference on Research in English and the National Council of Teachers of English.

ISER, W. (1980). The reading process: A phenomenological approach. In J.P. Tompkins (Ed.), *Reader response criticism: From formalism to poststructuralism* (pp. 50–69). Baltimore, MD: Johns Hopkins University Press.

JOHNSON, D.W., & JOHNSON, R.T. (1979). Conflict in the classroom: Controversy and learning. *Review of Educational Research, 49*, 51–70.

JOHNSTON, P.H. (1983). *Reading comprehension assessment: A cognitive basis*. Newark, DE: International Reading Association.

LANGER, J.A. (1992). Rethinking literature instruction. In J.A. Langer (Ed.), *Literature instruction: A focus on student response* (pp. 35–53). Urbana, IL: National Council of Teachers of English.

LANGER, J.A., APPLEBEE, A.N., MULLIS, I.V.S., & FOERTSCH, M.A. (1990). *Learning to read in our nation's schools: Instruction and achievement in 1988 at grades 4, 8, and 12*. Princeton, NJ: Educational Testing Service.

LEAL, D. (1992). The nature of talk about three types of text during peer group discussions. *Journal of Reading Behavior, 24*(3), 313–338.

MANDLER, J.M., & JOHNSON, N.S. (1977). Remembrance of things parsed: Story structure and recall. *Cognitive Psychology, 9*, 111–157.

MANY, J.E., & WISEMAN, D.L. (1992). The effect of teaching approach on third-grade students' response to literature. *Journal of Reading Behavior, 24*(3), 265–287.

MARTINEZ, M., ROSER, N.L., HOFFMAN, J.V., & BATTLE, J. (1992). Fostering better book discussions through response logs and a response framework: A case of description. In C.K. Kinzer & D.J. Leu (Eds.), *Literacy research, theory, and practice: Views from many perspectives* (41st Yearbook of the National Reading Conference, pp. 303–311). Chicago, IL: National Reading Conference.

MCGEE, L. (1992). An exploration of meaning construction in first graders' grand conversations. In C.K. Kinzer & D.J. Leu (Eds.), *Literacy research, theory, and practice: Views from many perspectives* (41st Yearbook of the National Reading Conference, pp. 177-186). Chicago, IL: National Reading Conference.

MCMAHON, S. (1992). *A group of five students as they participate in their student-led book club*. Unpublished doctoral dissertation, Michigan State University, East Lansing, MI.

MEHAN, H. (1979). *Learning lessons*. Cambridge, MA: Harvard University Press.

MORROW, L.M., & WEINSTEIN, C.S. (1986). Encouraging voluntary reading: The impact of a literature program on children's use of library corners. *Reading Research Quarterly, 21*, 330–346.

MUGNY, G., & DOISE, W. (1978). Socio-cognitive conflict and structure of individual and collective performances. *European Journal of Social Psychology, 8*, 181–192.

O'FLAHAVAN, J.F. (1989). *An exploration of the effects of participant structure upon literacy development in reading group discussion*. Unpublished doctoral dissertation, University of Illinois, Urbana-Champaign.

ORSOLINI, M., & PONTECORVO, C. (1992). Children's talk in classroom discussions. *Cognition and Instruction, 9*(2), 113–136.

PRAWAT, R. (1989). Promoting access to knowledge, strategy, and disposition in students: A research synthesis. *Review of Educational Research, 59*(1), 1–41.

PRESSLEY, M., EL-DINARY, P.B., GASKINS, I., SCHUDER, T., BERGMAN, J., ALMASI, J.F., & BROWN, R. (1992). Beyond direct explanation: Transactional instruction of reading comprehension strategies. *The Elementary School Journal, 92*(5), 513–555.

ROGOFF, B. (1990). *Apprenticeship in thinking: Cognitive development in social context*. New York: Oxford University Press.

ROSENBLATT, L.M. (1938/1976). *Literature as exploration*. New York: Modern Language Association.

ROSENBLATT, L.M. (1978). *The reader, the text, the poem: The transactional theory of the literary work*. Carbondale, IL: Southern Illinois University Press.

SLAVIN, R.E. (1990). *Cooperative learning: Theory, research, and practice*. Englewood Cliffs, NJ: Prentice-Hall.

STEIN, N.C., & GLENN, C.G. (1979). An analysis of story comprehension in elementary school children. In

R. O. Freedle (Ed.), *New directions in discourse processing* (pp. 53–120). Norwood, NJ: Ablex.

SWEIGART, W. (1991). Classroom talk, knowledge development, and writing. *Research in the Teaching of English, 25*(4), 469–496.

VYGOTSKY, L.S. (1978). *Mind in Society.* Cambridge, MA: Harvard University Press.

WEBB, N.M., & PALINCSAR, A.S. (in press). Group processes in the classroom. In D. Berliner & R. Calfee (Eds.), *Handbook of research in educational psychology.* New York: Macmillan.

Children's Literature References

FLEISCHMAN, S. (1989). McBroom tells the truth. In B.E. Cullinan, R.C. Farr, W.D. Hammond, N.L. Roser, & D.S. Strickland (Eds.), *Crossroads* (pp. 765–788). Orlando, FL: Harcourt Brace Jovanovich.

LEVY, E. (1986). Something strange at the ballpark. In V.A. Arnold & C.B. Smith (Eds.), *Winning moments* (pp. 127–140). New York: Macmillan.

NIXON, J.L. (1989). If you say so Claude. In B.E. Cullinan, R.C. Farr, W.D. Hammond, N.L. Roser, & D.S. Strickland (Eds.), *Crossroads* (pp. 239–254). Orlando, FL: Harcourt Brace Jovanovich.

PECK, R.N. (1986). Soup's new shoes. In V.A. Arnold & C.B. Smith (Eds.), *Winning moments* (pp. 276–286). New York: Macmillan.

SOBOL, D. (1986). The case of the crowing rooster. In V.A. Arnold & C.B. Smith (Eds.), *Winning moments* (pp. 346–352). New York: Macmillan.

STRETE, C.K. (1986). Grandfather and rolling thunder. In V.A. Arnold & C.B. Smith (Eds.), *Winning moments* (pp. 343–362). New York: Macmillan.

CHAPTER 2

What Research Reveals About Discussion

Linda B. Gambrell

> A traditional homily tells us that fish would be the least likely creatures to ever become aware of water. For those of us who teach, talk surrounds us and it also constitutes our primary mode of action. It is our medium, our atmosphere, and also our substance. And it is therefore invisible to us much of the time. Because talk is invisible to us, we rarely treat it as a matter of deliberate concern for teaching and learning.
>
> Rubin, 1990, p.5

The three purposes of this chapter are to present a brief rationale for the current resurgence of interest in the role of discussion in the reading and language arts curriculum, to place discussion in proper perspective with respect to other kinds of verbal interactions, and to summarize what research reveals about discussion. The research on discussion is reviewed along two lines, first with particular emphasis on how engaging in discussion helps students learn, and second, on factors that influence discussion.

MAKING DISCUSSION VISIBLE

This chapter focuses on research conducted primarily in elementary classrooms in order to describe what we know about the effects of discussion on student learning. It is important for us to understand how discussion contributes to learning because of the skill, time, and effort that are necessary for creating classroom cultures that foster engagement in discussion. How does discussion facilitate learning? Is it worth the time and effort? What teacher behaviors facilitate discussion? These are questions that researchers and educators have pondered for centuries.

> *Discussion brings together listening, speaking, and thinking skills as participants engage in exchanging ideas, responding, and reacting to text as well as to the ideas of others.*

Currently there is a resurgence of interest in small group discussion, particularly as it relates to reading comprehension and learning from text. As evidenced by the number of recent articles in literacy journals describing current classroom practices related to small group discussion, and recent research exploring the effects of discussion on student outcomes, it is clear that discussion is becoming increasingly more visible in both our educational literature and our classrooms (Barton, 1995; Commeyras, 1994; Horowitz & Freeman, 1995; Roller & Beed, 1994; Villaume & Hopkins, 1995; Villaume, Worden, Williams, Hopkins, & Rosenblatt, 1994; Wiencek & O'Flahavan, 1994).

Any attempt to review the research on discussion must begin by examining the nature and definition of discussion itself. Educational theorists and researchers often present a view of discussion that is idealized as something that should be strived for because it allows for greater student expression and involvement and results in increased learning. Furthermore, this idealized model is usually part of a Vygotskian framework that views social interaction as effectively driving cognitive development (Vygotsky, 1978). Within this framework, discussion is essentially dialogic: it is not completely controlled by a single participant; rather it occurs as natural conversation in which individuals engage in a free and open exchange of ideas. According to Lindfors (1990), effective discussions are an "ongoing process of inviting and sustaining children's talk and response...as they carry out their deepest human urgings: to connect with others, to understand their world, and to reveal themselves within it" (p. 38).

A Resurgence of Interest in Discussion

The resurgence of interest in discussion may be attributed to current theories and practices in reading and language arts. First, there is increasing evidence that teachers are now making greater use of literature in the reading and language arts program than ever before (Gambrell, 1992; Strickland, 1995). Moreover, literature is particularly appropriate for use with a wide range of student-centered activities that include response to and interpretation of what an author has written. Therefore, in classrooms where literature is the foundation of the reading program, discussion takes on a more important role as students participate in literature circles, idea circles, book clubs, and reader-response groups.

A second reason for the increasing interest in discussion is the emphasis on the meaningful integration of the language arts. Discussion brings together listening, speaking, and thinking skills as participants engage in exchanging ideas, responding, and reacting to text as well as to the ideas of others.

A third reason is that current theories of learning view students as active learners who engage in the construction of knowledge. These theories suggest that the primary goal of instruction is to help students construct personal meanings in response to new experiences rather than to simply learn the meanings others have created (Poplin, 1988). A fourth reason for the current focus on discussion is the clear link between discussion and the social construction of knowledge. Meaning making is learned through the social interactions of students, especially when they discuss and interpret text in small groups. Ways of meaning making are made public as students observe and participate in discussions about text. According to Straw and Bogdan (1993), engaging in discussions about text can help students become part of the "active conversation that *is* reading, the conversation between the reader and text, between text and community and among readers" (p. 4).

THE PLACE OF DISCUSSION IN THE CONTINUUM OF TALK

Rubin (1990) suggests that one way to describe talk is to think about the range of audiences with whom we can interact. He points out that this widening circle of interactants ranges from talking to ourselves to talking to large audiences. For example, we can engage in intrapersonal communication which is characterized as inner speech or talking to ourselves. When we talk to another person one-on-one, it is characterized as personal conversation. If the conversation includes several individuals we know, it is characterized as small group discussion. When we participate with a larger group of people where there is a definite separation and inequality between the roles of speaker and listener, talk is characterized as public communication or recitation. In this case, one person monologues while the others in the group do not (see Almasi, this volume, for a description of recitations). Finally, when talk is mediated by technology so that there is no definite way of knowing which members of the audience are "tuned in" to the message, it is characterized as broadcasting.

The model of talk presented in Figure 1 draws upon and extends Rubin's (1990) categorization scheme for types of talk. It provides a view of talk that considers several important dimensions of communication. First, talk can be viewed on a continuum of informal to formal talk; second, it can also be consid-

> "*Response-ability requires social interactions centered around text.*"

Figure 1
A model of the continuum of talk.

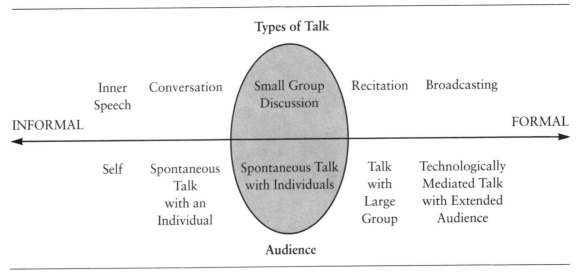

Types of Talk

	Inner Speech	Conversation	Small Group Discussion	Recitation	Broadcasting	
INFORMAL						FORMAL
	Self	Spontaneous Talk with an Individual	Spontaneous Talk with Individuals	Talk with Large Group	Technologically Mediated Talk with Extended Audience	

Audience

ered with respect to different types of talk; and third, it can be viewed in terms of the audiences being addressed. In the model presented in Figure 1, it is worth noting that small group discussion falls in the middle of the continuum of talk, between the informal and more formal modes of communication. Just as small group discussion is the "centerpiece" of the continuum of talk, it is also the central focus of this book. When students engage in small group discussions they have more opportunities to speak, interact, interpret, clarify, and exchange points of view than are afforded in other talk structures.

In the past, typical classroom discussions relied heavily on the public communication or recitation models of interaction, with the teacher as the transmitter of information. Teachers talked and asked questions and students listened and answered teacher-posed questions (White, 1990). This type of teacher-centered instruction provides students with few opportunities to enter into the dialogue of learning. The teacher controls the timing, the structure, and the content of classroom talk, allowing students limited opportunities to develop what Rubin (1990) has referred to as "response-ability."

DISCUSSION AS RESPONSE-ABILITY

If students are to develop critical and creative thinking skills, they must have opportunities to respond to text. The ability to respond to text, or response-ability, is socially mediated and is learned through a process of socialization in the literacy community. Thus, response-ability is nurtured when students have opportunities to negotiate meaning with text and with other members of the interpretive community. By its very nature, response-ability requires social interactions centered around text. In many ways, response-ability reflects the Vygotskian (1978) perspective that the ways in which we think are learned through our social interactions. According to Straw and Bogdan (1993), this perspective "argues for socially based classrooms, classrooms that lead students to the negotiations that are the heart of meaning making in the act of reading" (p. 4).

"When students engage in small group discussions they have more opportunities to speak, interact, interpret, clarify, and exchange points of view than are afforded in other talk structures."

In many of today's classrooms, students participate more fully in the dialogue of learning as they engage in small group discussions about what they have read. In particular, the research on collaborative learning has encouraged teachers to provide more opportunities for students to work and interact in small groups (Slavin, 1989, 1990). Students are more likely to be involved in collaborative projects and small group discussions where they engage in problem solving and creative thinking. Students are also more likely to be involved in decision making about who talks and about what is discussed during small group discussions. Conversely, teachers are more likely to view themselves as coaches or facilitators who are there to nurture and support children who engage in fruitful and meaningful discussions. This new view of the role of discussion in today's classroom is one in which students have increased opportunities to develop response-ability and higher level thinking skills.

WHAT RESEARCH REVEALS ABOUT DISCUSSION AND STUDENT LEARNING

Much of the existing research on the topic of discussion has centered on the recitation model, and the majority of this research has been conducted with teachers and students at the secondary level (Alvermann, 1986; Alvermann, O'Brien, & Dillon, 1990). Only recently has research begun to focus specifically on small group discussion and its effects on elementary age students' learning (Almasi, 1995; Wiencek & O'Flahavan, 1994). This emerging body of research suggests that there are many positive educational outcomes associated with using small group discussion in elementary classrooms (Gall, 1987; Gall & Gall, 1976, 1990; Gall & Gillett, 1980). In the following section, a brief review of the research is presented which suggests that engaging in discussion about text results in deeper understanding, higher level thinking, and improved communication skills.

DISCUSSION PROMOTES DEEP UNDERSTANDING OF TEXT. A number of research studies on discussion have found that positive effects accrue when children engage in small group discussions about text. Research documents that discussion enhances text recall, aesthetic response to text, and reading comprehension.

Research by Palincsar (1987) and Palincsar and Brown (1984) supports the contention that discussion is an effective method for promoting deep understanding of text. Reading is one of the primary means by which children acquire information. While most children can decode and grasp the meaning of passages they read, many children still have difficulty comprehending text. Palincsar developed and researched the technique of reciprocal teaching that involves students in structured discussions. In reciprocal teaching, a student volunteers to take the role of the teacher and questions other students about what has been read. Other group members are also encouraged to ask questions and make comments. Students engage in asking questions of four types: (a) that ask about important information in the text, (b) that ask for a summary of the text, (c) that ask for clarification of the text, and (d) that ask for predictions about upcoming events or specific content in the text. The results of Palincsar's study revealed that the reciprocal teaching group outperformed comparison groups on reading comprehension.

In Morrow and Smith's (1990) study of kindergarten students, children who engaged in small group discussions of stories that were read aloud had superior story recall compared to students who discussed the story one-on-one with the teacher or participated in whole class discussions. Furthermore, the research of Eeds and Wells (1989) documents the high quality of children's aesthetic responses to text during discussions. Children in their study engaged in constructing meaning and personal interpretation of text, and they modified their interpretations of text as a result of interactions with other group members. Taken together, these studies support the effectiveness of discussion in promoting students' deeper understanding of text.

DISCUSSION INCREASES HIGHER LEVEL THINKING AND PROBLEM-SOLVING ABILITY. Several studies have explored the effects of discussion on the higher level thinking and problem-solving ability of elementary age students. Hudgins and Edelman (1986) examined the effects of participation in small group discussions on the critical thinking of fourth and fifth grade students. Critical thinking was defined as the disposition to provide supporting evidence of a student's conclusions and to request evidence from others before accepting conclusions. Teachers were taught how to reduce the amount of teacher talk in discussion and to encourage students to take responsibility for thinking and talking during discussions. Although there were no significant differences between the experimental group and a control group on a test of critical thinking, an analysis of the discussions revealed that students in the experimental group provided more supporting evidence for conclusions during the discussions as compared to the control group.

A study conducted by Almasi (1995) compared student-led and teacher-led discussion groups. One of the major findings of this study was that in student-led discussions, which allowed the students a more participatory role in the interpretation of text, students engaged in higher level thinking and problem solving. One explanation for this finding is that student-led discussions allow students to try their own thinking and engage in exploratory thinking, resulting in more extended and more elaborate mental representations and higher level analytical thinking. In addition, Almasi (1995) found that student-led discussions resulted in more extensive and higher level discussions than teacher-led discussions. Likewise, the student-led discussions were typified by more student talk, higher level thinking, wider participation from group members, greater cohesion within the group, and richer inquiry.

" Student-led discussions allow students to try their own thinking and engage in exploratory thinking, resulting in more extended and more elaborate mental representations and higher level analytical thinking. "

Studies by Villaume and Hopkins (1995) and Green and Wallet (1981) document ways that students interact with each other during small group discussions. These studies provide numerous examples of how discussion stimulates and serves as a scaffold for students' thinking. In addition, these studies support research showing that in-depth critical thinking is developed through discussion and suggest the need for small group discussion rather than having students respond primarily to teacher questions (Almasi, 1995; Morrow & Smith, 1990).

DISCUSSION IMPROVES COMMUNICATION SKILLS. Recent research by Almasi (1995) and Eeds & Wells (1989) indicates that students' communication skills improve naturally as they become more experienced in small group discussions. Studies on discussion have documented increases in communication behaviors such as the occurrence of student-to-student interaction, recognition and acknowledgment of the previous speaker, requesting verification, and the ability to take on a position different from their own (Almasi, 1995; Goatley & Raphael, 1992; Phillips, 1973).

Discussion has also been a means of helping students develop socially desirable attitudes. For example, discussion can provide students with exposure to information that can change their attitudes or intensify existing attitudes. In a study conducted by Fisher (1968), fifth grade students were randomly assigned to one of three treatment groups. One group read a series of stories designed to promote positive attitudes toward Native Americans; the second group read the same stories and participated in a discussion after reading; the third group served as a control group that neither read the stories nor discussed Native Americans. The major finding from this study was that discussion caused significantly more attitudinal changes as compared to the other two treatment groups, resulting in more positive attitudes toward Native Americans for the group that participated in discussions.

Discussions also help students to develop what Slavin (1977) has called "social connectedness." Engaging students in cooperative learning groups that emphasize discussion and interaction has been found to have positive effects on interracial friendships and interracial attitudes (Slavin, 1977, 1989, 1990). When students are encouraged and supported in interacting with their classmates in small group discussions, they have opportunities to develop the skills and behaviors needed to communicate and work effectively with others.

WHAT RESEARCH REVEALS ABOUT FACTORS THAT AFFECT DISCUSSION

New research reveals a clearer picture of what effective discussion looks like and sounds like. We now know that the quality of discussion is affected by factors such as group size, leadership, text type, and cultural background. In addition, research supports the notion that even young children can engage in and learn from participation in discussion groups and that children with special needs also benefit from engaging in discussion.

DISCUSSION IS INFLUENCED BY TEXT TYPE. Only a few studies to date have explored the relationship between content or text type (narrative or expository) on children's discussions. Leal (1992) conducted a studythat investigated the effect of text type on the quality of children's discussions of stories. Children in grades one, three, and five were assigned to one of three treatment groups where they listened to either a storybook, an information book, or an informational storybook. The informational storybook was based on information but was presented in a narrative format (for example, the *Magic School Bus* series). Results of this study revealed important differences for both grade level and text type. As expected, older students were more successful at collaboration and relied more on peer comments in their discussion. The major finding of the study was that informational storybooks enhanced discussion more than narrative or expository texts. Students across all grade levels offered more speculations and relied more on the comments of peers when discussing the informational storybook as compared to either of the other two text

> " *The quality of discussion is affected by factors such as group size, leadership, text type, and cultural background.* "

types. The results of this study suggest that the quality and texture of text-based discussion is influenced by text type.

In a study with kindergartners and second graders, Horowitz and Freeman (1995) found that discussion can play an influential role in students' preference, sense of difficulty, and understanding of author's purpose when asked to process science texts. This study compared discussion before and after listening to two science texts with a no discussion condition. When they engaged in discussion, children in this study preferred an informational science book over a narrative science book. When there was no discussion and the book was simply read to the children, they preferred the narrative science book. In addition, the children perceived the books that were discussed to be easier, and they had better comprehension of the books that were discussed. Horowitz and Freeman (1995) concluded that discussion can create a conceptual change about text and can result in a preference for a text that students initially find to be of limited interest or appeal. This research suggests that discussions have the potential for increasing children's curiosity, broadening their interest, and restructuring their preferences for text.

DISCUSSION IS INFLUENCED BY GROUP SIZE. A relatively large number of studies provide information about the effect of group size on the quality and outcomes of discussion and suggest that small group discussions provide individual students with more opportunities to speak. Wiencek and O'Flahavan (1994) indicate that group size should be large enough to ensure diversity of ideas, yet small enough so that each student has an opportunity to fully participate. In an analysis of 10 research studies investigating small group discussions with kindergarten and elementary age students, Spence (1993) found that the range of small group size was from 3 to 14 participants and that most researchers defined a "small group" as five or six students.

In a classic study with kindergarten students, Morrow and Smith (1990) compared the following group structures: one-to-one (student/teacher), small groups of 3 students, and whole class (15 students). The children in these groups listened to a story and then discussed it. Assessment was conducted using free recalls of the story. The results revealed that the small group structure yielded significantly superior story recall as compared to the other two group structures. Morrow and Smith (1990) concluded that the small group discussion structure facilitates literacy development because students have more opportunity to speak, interact, discuss, and exchange points of view than in other group structures. Other studies conducted with elementary age to high school age students provide consistent and compelling evidence in support of the superior quality of discussions that areconducted within the small group structure (Davidson, 1985; Palincsar, Brown, & Martin, 1987; Rogers, 1991; Sweigart, 1991).

> **" *Leadership affects the interaction patterns and the level of thinking that transpires during discussions.* "**

DISCUSSION IS INFLUENCED BY LEADERSHIP. Most of the studies on discussion involve a teacher or researcher who acts as a group leader, actually taking part in the group interaction. Some studies have examined only student-led discussions (Goatley & Raphael, 1992; Short, 1992), and others have compared teacher-led versus student-led discussions (Almasi, 1995; Wiseman, et al., 1992). The results of these studies indicate that the leadership (teacher-led, student-led, or shared leadership) affects the interaction patterns and the level of thinking that transpires during discussions. The discussions are most productive and students are more engaged in discussions when the teacher serves as a guide and facilitator to help children gain interpretive authority. Thus, a number of studies have involved training either students (Goatley & Raphael, 1992; Martinez, et al., 1992), teachers (Palincsar, 1986), or both students and teachers (Almasi, 1995; Wiseman et al., 1992) in order to create a discussion structure in which students have real control and authority.

Several studies have suggested that teachers play an important role in supporting students in the development of discussion skills as well as the development of higher level thinking skills. The research of O'Flahavan and his colleagues (1992) suggests that if teachers remove themselves completely from influencing the discussion process, it is likely that children's responses to literature will not develop and grow. McGee's (1992) research with first graders indicates that although it is important for children to explore stories on their own terms, teachers can facilitate higher level discussion by focusing the conversation around a teacher-posed interpretive question.

Clearly, students profit from having the freedom to explore their own agendas during discussions; however, it appears that they also profit from teacher guidance. Students need the freedom to express divergent ideas and interpretations of text, but they also need some direction in how to move toward more interpretative or critical stances with respect to their reading of text. Thus, teachers play a significant role in guiding students toward higher level discussions as they engage in modeling behavior, providing frameworks for approaching texts, and posing interpretive questions.

DISCUSSION IS INFLUENCED BY THE CULTURAL BACKGROUND OF THE PARTICIPANTS. Although few studies have specifically addressed the influence of cultural background on discussion, numerous anthropological studies of classroom discourse suggest that students of minority cultures often find themselves struggling to make sense of interaction patterns that occur in the classroom context (White, 1990). This is of paramount concern because many of our minority students (black, Latino, Native American, and Hawaiian) have low reading achievement scores (National Center for Education Statistics, 1988, 1992). Students of all cultures come to the classroom with considerable language strengths; however, unless these strengths are recognized and acknowledged, students may have difficulty engaging in classroom learning.

Heath's (1983) study of children from a southeastern U.S. town revealed that questions were used differently by young black students and their teachers. The children did not respond to "known answer" questions. They would lapse into silence or contribute minimal information when teachers asked direct factual questions. However, when the questions asked of the children were more authentic and representative of the kinds of questions posed to them in their home and community environment, these children responded actively and aggressively, offering useful information about their past experiences. Heath concluded that an awareness and use of the kinds of language that children use in the home and community can foster interaction and discussion in the school setting.

According to Delpit (1990) "one of the most difficult tasks we face as human beings is communicating meaning across our individual differences, a task confounded immeasurably when we attempt to communicate across social lines, racial lines, cultural lines or lines of unequal power" (p. 263). Anthropological analyses of cultural differences during discussion can lead to the identification of students' language strengths and ways to engage all students in successful classroom discussions (White, 1990).

CONCLUSIONS

Clearly, discussion can make an important and unique contribution to helping children learn from text. The research on small group discussion in elementary classrooms supports the notion that such interaction engages students in the co-construction of knowledge, advances student learning, and provides opportunities for students to learn important interpersonal skills while conversing, interpreting, and negotiating in active and constructive ways. There is no one method or approach for implementing the ideal discussion; instead, research suggests that teachers have important choices to make. Future research is needed to illuminate how text type, group size, leadership, and group composition affect discussion. Yet ultimately, the creation of effective, small group discussions within the classroom context is a process of experimentation and refinement in order to find the most appropriate approach to fit students' needs.

Author's Note

I would like to express my appreciation to Bill Spence and Beth Holmberg for their contributions to this chapter, and in particular, I would like to acknowledge their insights about what research reveals about discussion. Also, I extend my appreciation to Susan Mazzoni for her careful reading and her creative contributions to the final draft.

References

ALMASI, J.F. (1996). A new view of discussion. In L.B. Gambrell & J.F. Almasi (Eds.), *Lively discussions!: Fostering engaged reading.* Newark, DE: International Reading Association.

ALMASI, J.F. (1995). The nature of fourth graders' sociocognitive conflicts in peer-led and teacher-led discussions of literature. *Reading Research Quarterly, 30,* 314–351.

ALVERMANN, D.E. (1986). Discussion versus recitation in the secondary classroom. In J.A. Niles & R.V. Lalik (Eds.), *Solving problems in literacy: Learners, teachers, and researchers.* Rochester, NY: National Reading Conference.

ALVERMANN, D.E., O'BRIEN, D.G., & DILLON, D.R. (1990). What teachers do when they say they're having discussions of content area reading assignments: A qualitative analysis. *Reading Research Quarterly, 25,* 296–322.

BARTON, J. (1995). Conducting effective classroom discussions. *Journal of Reading, 38,* 346–350.

COMMEYRAS, M. (1994). Were Janell and Neesi in the same classroom? Questions as the first order of reality in storybook discussions. *Language Arts, 71,* 517–523.

DAVIDSON, J.L. (1985). What you think is going on, isn't: Eighth grade students' introspections of discussions in science and social studies lessons. In J.A. Niles & R.V. Lalik (Eds.), *Issues in literacy: A research perspective* (pp. 238–243). Rochester, NY: National Reading Conference.

DELPIT, L.D. (1990). Language diversity and learning. In S. Hynds & D.L. Rubin (Eds.), *Perspectives on talk and learning* (pp. 247–266). Urbana, IL: National Council of Teachers of English.

EEDS, M., & WELLS, D. (1989). Grand conversations: an exploration of meaning construction in literature study groups. *Research in the Teaching of English, 23,* 4–29.

FISHER, F.L. (1968). The influence of reading and discussion on the attitudes of fifth graders toward Indians. *Journal of Education Research, 62,* 130–134.

GALL, J.P., & GALL, M.D. (1990). Outcomes of the discussion method. In W.W. Wilen (Ed.), *Teaching and learning through discussion* (pp. 25–44). Springfield, IL: Charles C. Thomas.

GALL, M.D. (1987). Discussion methods. In M.J. Dunkin (Ed.), *The international encyclopedia of teaching and teacher education* (pp. 232–237). Oxford, UK: Pergamon.

GALL, M.D., & GALL, J.R. (1976). The discussion method. In N.L. Gage (Ed.), *Psychology of teaching methods.* (National Society for the Study of Education, 75th Yearbook, Part 1, pp. 166–216). Chicago, IL: University of Chicago Press.

GALL, M.D., & GILLETT, M. (1980). The discussion method in classroom teaching. *Theory into Practice, 19,* 98–103.

GAMBRELL, L.B. (1992). Elementary school literacy: Changes and challenges. In M.J. Dreher & W.H. Slater (Eds.), *Elementary school literacy: Critical issues,* (pp. 227–239). Norwood, MA: Christopher-Gordon.

GOATLEY, V.J., & RAPHAEL, T.E. (1992). Non-traditional learners' written and dialogic response to literature. In C.K. Kinzer & D.J. Leu (Eds.), *Literacy research, theory, and practice: Views from many perspectives* (pp. 313–322). Chicago, IL: National Reading Conference.